I SAY I'M SORRY

BY CHARLOTTE TAYLOR

Gareth Stevens
PUBLISHING

Please visit our website, www.garethstevens.com. For a free color catalog of all our high-quality books, call toll free 1-800-542-2595 or fax 1-877-542-2596.

Cataloging-in-Publication Data
Names: Taylor, Charlotte.
Title: Yo pido disculpas / Charlotte Taylor.
Description: New York : Gareth Stevens Publishing, 2021. | Series: Tenemos carácter | Includes glossary and index.
Identifiers: ISBN 9781538260791 (pbk.) | ISBN 9781538260814 (library bound) | ISBN 9781538260807 (6 pack) | ISBN 9781538260821 (ebook)
Subjects: LCSH: Apologizing–Juvenile literature. | Children–Conduct of life–Juvenile literature.
Classification: LCC BF575.A75 T39 2021 | DDC 395–dc23

Published in 2021 by
Gareth Stevens Publishing
111 East 14th Street, Suite 349
New York, NY 10003

Designer: Sarah Liddell
Editor: Megan Quick

Photo credits: Cover, p. 1 spass/Shutterstock.com; background throughout Igor Vitkovskiy/Shutterstock.com; p. 5 VGstockstudio/Shutterstock.com; p. 7 Robert Kneschke/Shutterstock.com; p. 9 tammykayphoto/Shutterstock.com; p. 11 Dan76/Shutterstock.com; pp. 13, 19 pixelheadphoto digitalskillet/Shutterstock.com; p. 15 Brocreative/Shutterstock.com; p. 17 antoniodiaz/Shutterstock.com; p. 21 Monkey Business Images/Shutterstock.com.

Printed in the United States of America

Some of the images in this book illustrate individuals who are models. The depictions do not imply actual situations or events.

CPSIA compliance information: Batch #CS20GS: For further information contact Gareth Stevens, New York, New York at 1-800-542-2595.

Find us on

CONTENTS

Boldface words appear in the glossary.

When Do I Say I'm Sorry?

Sometimes we have to say we're sorry. Maybe we did something unkind. Maybe we hurt someone by **accident**. We should still say we're sorry. We can also try to make it better. Saying we're sorry shows that we care about how others feel.

Clean It Up

Theo **knocked** over a cup of water on Carter's desk. It spilled all over Carter's paper. Theo didn't mean to do it. He told Carter that he was sorry. Then he helped Carter clean up the mess.

Pay It Back

Isaac and his friends were playing baseball in the street. Isaac hit a ball into his neighbor's window. The window broke! Isaac rang the neighbor's doorbell and told him he was sorry. He also said he would help pay for the window.

Jackie found a cake on the kitchen table. She ate a big piece. Her mom was upset. She had made the cake for a bake sale. Jackie said she was sorry. Then she helped her mom bake another cake.

Naomi borrowed her sister's **necklace**. She wore it to the mall. When Naomi got home, it was gone. Oh no! She had lost the necklace. Naomi told her sister she was sorry. Naomi saved her money to buy a new one.

Be Kind

Wyatt and Henry had a **sleepover**. Wyatt slept with a teddy bear. At school, Henry told their friends about Wyatt's toy. Some of them made fun of Wyatt. Henry felt bad and told them to stop. He told Wyatt he was sorry.

15

I Get Mad

Emilia was having a bad day. When Jack took the toy she was playing with, she got angry and hit him. Jack started to cry. Emilia took a deep breath. She knew that hitting was wrong. She told Jack she was sorry.

Tell the Truth

Zachary was watching TV. His dad asked him if he had done his homework. Zachary said yes. But he hadn't done it. Later, Zachary felt bad. He told his dad the truth. He said he was sorry he hadn't been **honest**.

It Takes Two

Ellie wore her new dress to a party. Madison spilled her drink on it. Ellie yelled at Madison. The next day, Madison told Ellie she was sorry. Then Ellie said she was sorry too. Sometimes both people should say they're sorry.

GLOSSARY

accident: something unexpected that happens by chance

honest: truthful

knock: to hit against

necklace: a piece of jewelry worn around the neck

sleepover: an overnight stay

FOR MORE INFORMATION

BOOKS

Dyckman, Ame. *Horrible Bear!* New York, NY: Little, Brown, & Co., 2016.

Verde, Susan. *I Am Human: A Book of Empathy.* New York, NY: Abrams Books for Young Readers, 2018.

WEBSITES

PBS Kids: Saying I'm Sorry Is the First Step
pbskids.org/video/daniel-tigers-neighborhood/2365019278
A fun song explores when and how to say sorry.

Your Feelings: I'm Sorry
www.cyh.com/HealthTopics/HealthTopicDetailsKids.aspx?p=335&np=287&id=2686#4
This website gives examples of situations and suggestions for how to say you are sorry.

INDEX